Wee Sing®

presents

OVER IN THE MEADOW

a musical story/play

A Wee Sing book by
Pamela Conn Beall and Susan Hagen Nipp

Story by
Kathy Fahlman Bates and Dorothy Pederson Fahlman

Illustrated by
Charles E. Reasoner

PRICE/STERN/SLOAN
Publishers, Inc., Los Angeles

Acknowledgements

"OVER IN THE MEADOW" words by Olive Wadsworth (1800's),
melody of unknown English origin.
WEE SING OVER IN THE MEADOW audiocassette produced by Cal Scott.

Dedication

To wee ones everywhere, especially Lindsay and Hilary.

Story copyright © 1987 by Kathy Fahlman Bates and Dorothy Pederson Fahlman
Illustrations copyright © 1987 by Charles E. Reasoner
Published by Price/Stern/Sloan Publishers, Inc.
360 North La Cienega Boulevard, Los Angeles, California 90048

ISBN 0-8431-1949-7

Preface

"Over in the Meadow" is a traditional song that lends itself to this charming story with a moral. It can be enjoyed simply as a story or, because of its easy script-like form, it can be expanded into an uncomplicated but delightful musical play for home or school.

If performed as a play, "Over in the Meadow" can be effective with or without props and costumes. If you do choose to use them, create some ideas with your child or children and let them help in the designing. You may want to use the following ideas to help get you started.

Draw and color some simple meadow props for the various habitats, such as the "sand in the sun" and the "stream runs blue." Cut them out and tape them to the floor or wall. Create masks or make paper bag or stick puppets to represent the various animals. Children's drawings work well for these. Be as simple or elaborate as your situation demands.

A delightful story, a simple play or an elaborate production — however you choose to use this musical story/play, a fun-filled experience awaits you!

Pam Beall
Susan Nipp

Cast

 Narrator

 Mother

 Billy

 Singers

 Mother Toad

 Little Toad

 Mother Fish

 Little Fish

 Mother Bluebird

 Little Bluebirds

 Mother Muskrat

 Little Muskrats

 Mother Honeybee

Little Honeybees

 Mother Crow

 Little Crows

 Mother Cricket

 Little Crickets

 Mother Lizard

 Little Lizards

 Mother Frog

 Little Frogs

 Mother Spider

 Little Spiders

The sun was shining and the flowers were in full bloom. It was a perfect day!

Billy was getting dressed when he heard his mother say . . .

 Billy, have you brushed your teeth?

 Why do I have to, Mother?

 Brushing keeps them healthy.

 I wish I were a . . . toad, then I wouldn't have to brush my teeth.

 Yes, but toads have to do other things.

 Like what?

 Let's go for a walk through the meadow and you can see for yourself.

 They walked and they walked until they came to a patch of sand in the sun. Looking closely, they saw a family of toads.

 Look, a mother toad and her little toadie one!

 Listen, I hear something!

They heard a song — a wonderful song!

1. O – ver in the mead-ow, in the sand in the sun, Lived an old moth-er toad - ie and her lit -tle toad - ie one. "Wink!" said the moth-er; "I wink!" said the one, So they winked and they blinked in the sand in the sun.

 Why should I wink, Mother?

Winking clears your eyes.

 Oh, now I understand!

Billy also understood. He waved good-bye to the toads as he and his mother continued on their way.

 They walked and they walked until they came to a place where the stream runs blue. Looking closely, they saw a family of fish.

 Look, a mother fish and her little fishes two!

 Listen, I hear something!

They heard a song — a wonderful song!

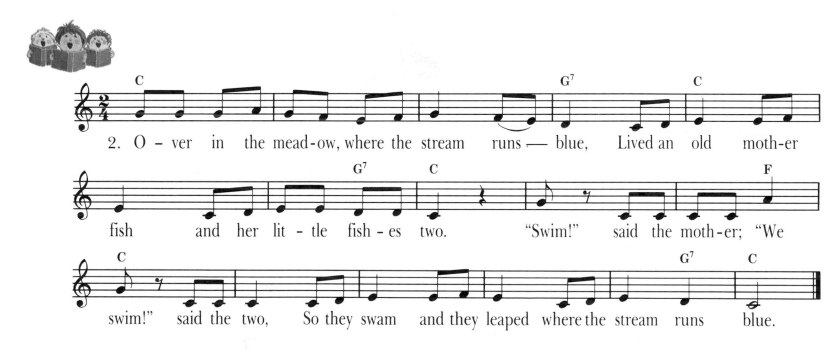

2. O – ver in the mead-ow, where the stream runs — blue, Lived an old moth-er fish and her lit – tle fish-es two. "Swim!" said the moth-er; "We swim!" said the two, So they swam and they leaped where the stream runs blue.

 Why should we swim, Mother?

 Swimming makes you strong.

 Oh, now we understand!

 Billy also understood. He waved good-bye to the fishes as he and his mother continued on their way.

 They walked and they walked until they came to a hole in a tree. Looking closely, they saw a family of bluebirds.

 Look, a mother bluebird and her little birdies three!

 Listen, I hear something!

They heard a song — a wonderful song!

3. O – ver in the mead-ow, in a hole in a tree, Lived an old moth-er blue-bird and her lit – tle bird – ies three. "Sing!" said the moth-er; "We sing!" said the three, So they sang and were glad in a hole in the tree.

 Why should we sing, Mother?

 Singing makes you happy.

 Oh, now we understand!

 Billy also understood. He waved good-bye to the bluebirds as he and his mother continued on their way.

 They walked and they walked until they came to some reeds on the shore. Looking closely, they saw a family of muskrats.

 Look, a mother muskrat and her little ratties four!

 Listen, I hear something!

They heard a song — a wonderful song!

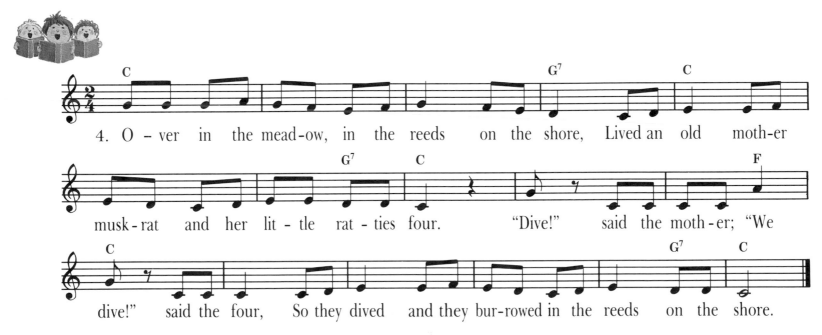

C   **G⁷**   **C**

4. O – ver in the mead-ow, in the reeds on the shore, Lived an old moth-er

G⁷   **C**   **F**

musk-rat and her lit – tle rat – ties four. "Dive!" said the moth-er; "We

C   **G⁷**   **C**

dive!" said the four, So they dived and they bur-rowed in the reeds on the shore.

Why should we dive, Mother?

Diving helps find food.

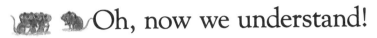Oh, now we understand!

Billy also understood. He waved good-bye to the muskrats as he and his mother continued on their way.

 They walked and they walked until they came to a snug beehive. Looking closely, they saw a family of honeybees.

 Look, a mother honeybee and her little bees five!

 Listen, I hear something!

They heard a song — a wonderful song!

C · G⁷ · C
5. O – ver in the mead-ow, in a snug bee —— hive, Lived a moth-er hon - ey

G⁷ · C · F
bee and her lit – tle bees five. "Buzz!" said the moth-er; "We

C · G⁷ · C
buzz!" said the five, So they buzzed and they hummed in the snug bee – hive.

 Why should we buzz, Mother?

 Buzzing means you're busy.

 Oh, now we understand!

 Billy also understood. He waved good-bye to the bees as he and his mother continued on their way.

 They walked and they walked until they came to a nest built of sticks. Looking closely, they saw a family of crows.

 Look, a mother crow and her little crows six!

 Listen, I hear something!

They heard a song — a wonderful song!

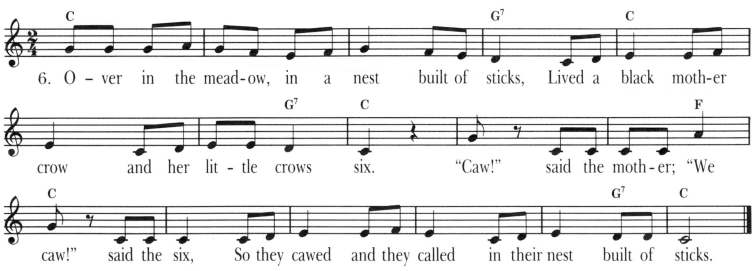

6. O – ver in the mead-ow, in a nest built of sticks, Lived a black moth-er crow and her lit-tle crows six. "Caw!" said the moth-er; "We caw!" said the six, So they cawed and they called in their nest built of sticks.

 Why should we caw, Mother?

 Cawing warns of danger.

 Oh, now we understand!

 Billy also understood. He waved good-bye to the crows as he and his mother continued on their way.

 They walked and they walked until they came to a spot where the grass was so even. Looking closely, they saw a family of crickets.

 Look, a mother cricket and her little crickets seven!

 Listen, I hear something!

They heard a song — a wonderful song!

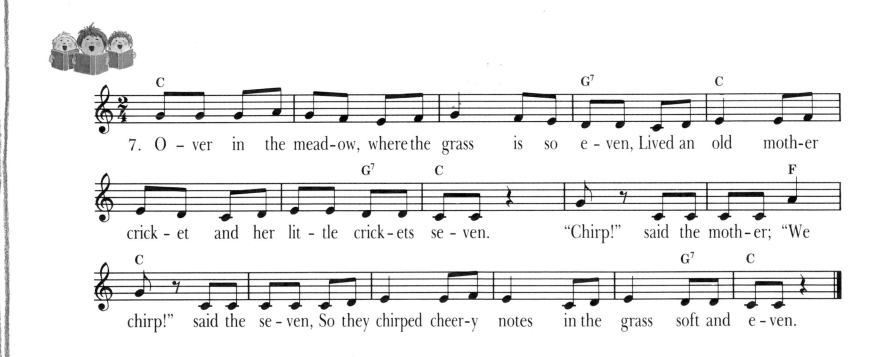

7. O – ver in the mead-ow, where the grass is so e - ven, Lived an old moth-er

crick - et and her lit - tle crick-ets se - ven. "Chirp!" said the moth-er; "We

chirp!" said the se - ven, So they chirped cheer-y notes in the grass soft and e - ven.

Why should we chirp, Mother?

Chirping keeps you cheery.

Oh, now we understand!

Billy also understood. He waved good-bye to the crickets as he and his mother continued on their way.

 They walked and they walked until they came to the old mossy gate. Looking closely, they saw a family of lizards.

 Look, a mother lizard and her little lizards eight!

 Listen, I hear something!

They heard a song — a wonderful song!

8. O – ver in the mead-ow, by the old mos-sy gate, Lived a brown moth-er liz – ard and her lit - tle liz-ards eight. "Bask!" said the moth-er; "We bask!" said the eight, So they basked in the sun on the old mos-sy gate.

Why should we bask, Mother?

Basking keeps you warm.

Oh, now we understand!

Billy also understood. He waved good-bye to the lizards as he and his mother continued on their way.

 They walked and they walked until they came to a place where the quiet pools shine. Looking closely, they saw a family of frogs.

 Look, a mother frog and her little froggies nine!

 Listen, I hear something!

They heard a song — a wonderful song!

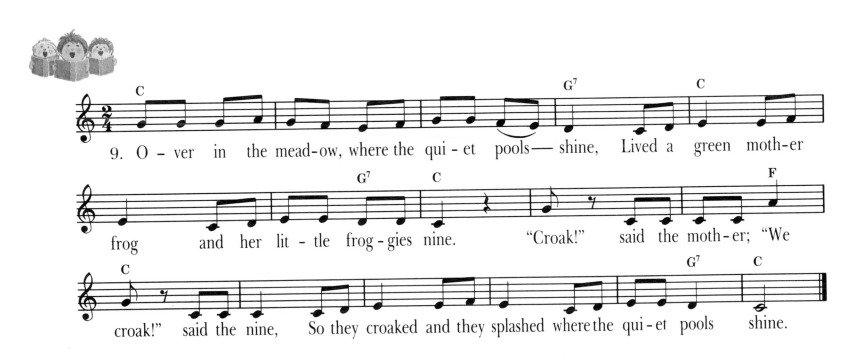

9. O – ver in the mead-ow, where the qui - et pools— shine, Lived a green moth-er frog and her lit - tle frog - gies nine. "Croak!" said the moth-er; "We croak!" said the nine, So they croaked and they splashed where the qui - et pools shine.

Why should we croak, Mother?

Croaking tells your thoughts.

Oh, now we understand!

Billy also understood. He waved good-bye to the frogs as he and his mother continued on their way.

 They walked and they walked until they came to a sly little den. Looking closely, they saw a family of spiders.

 Look, a mother spider and her little spiders ten!

 Listen, I hear something!

They heard a song — a wonderful song!

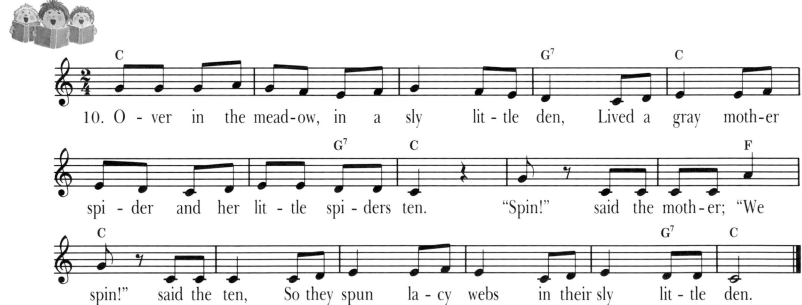

10. O - ver in the mead-ow, in a sly lit - tle den, Lived a gray moth-er spi - der and her lit - tle spi - ders ten. "Spin!" said the moth-er; "We spin!" said the ten, So they spun la - cy webs in their sly lit - tle den.

Why should we spin, Mother?

Spinning makes a web.

Oh, now we understand!

Billy also understood. He waved good-bye to the spiders. Now it was time for Billy and his mother to return home.

They crawled past the spiders,

leaped past the frogs,

tiptoed past the lizards,

jumped past the crickets,

flew past the crows,

ran past the bees,

skipped past the muskrats,

fluttered past the bluebirds,

swam past the fish

and hopped past the toads.

Finally, they were home!

 Billy had seen for himself that all children have things they need to do . . . and for good reasons, too!

Lyrics

1. Over in the meadow, in the sand in the sun,
   Lived an old mother toadie and her little toadie one.
   "Wink!" said the mother; "I wink!" said the one,
   So they winked and they blinked in the sand in the sun.

2. Over in the meadow, where the stream runs blue,
   Lived an old mother fish and her little fishes two.
   "Swim!" said the mother; "We swim!" said the two,
   So they swam and they leaped where the stream runs blue.

3. Over in the meadow, in a hole in a tree,
   Lived an old mother bluebird and her little birdies three.
   "Sing!" said the mother; "We sing!" said the three,
   So they sang and were glad in a hole in the tree.

4. Over in the meadow, in the reeds on the shore,
   Lived an old mother muskrat and her little ratties four.
   "Dive!" said the mother; "We dive!" said the four,
   So they dived and they burrowed in the reeds on the shore.

5. Over in the meadow, in a snug beehive,
   Lived a mother honey bee and her little bees five.
   "Buzz!" said the mother; "We buzz!" said the five,
   So they buzzed and they hummed in the snug beehive.

6. Over in the meadow, in a nest built of sticks,
   Lived a black mother crow and her little crows six.
   "Caw!" said the mother; "We caw!" said the six,
   So they cawed and they called in their nest built of sticks.

7. Over in the meadow, where the grass is so even,
   Lived an old mother cricket and her little crickets seven.
   "Chirp!" said the mother; "We chirp!" said the seven,
   So they chirped cheery notes in the grass soft and even.

8. Over in the meadow, by the old mossy gate,
   Lived a brown mother lizard and her little lizards eight.
   "Bask!" said the mother; "We bask!" said the eight,
   So they basked in the sun on the old mossy gate.

9. Over in the meadow, where the quiet pools shine,
   Lived a green mother frog and her little froggies nine.
   "Croak!" said the mother; "We croak!" said the nine,
   So they croaked and they splashed where the quiet pools shine.

10. Over in the meadow, in a sly little den,
    Lived a gray mother spider and her little spiders ten.
    "Spin!" said the mother; "We spin!" said the ten,
    So they spun lacy webs in their sly little den.

Over in the Meadow

piano accompaniment

arr. by D. Fahlman